# MARTYRS OF KOREA

by
Fr Richard Rutt

*All booklets are published thanks to the
generous support of the members of the
Catholic Truth Society*

## CATHOLIC TRUTH SOCIETY
PUBLISHERS TO THE HOLY SEE

# Contents

The Korean names in this story are pronounced with consonants as in English, vowels as in Italian. The sound for *ö* varies from that of *o* in 'word' to that of *o* in 'song'; and the sound for *ü* resembles that of *oo* in 'book'. The surname *Ch'oe* sounds like *chwè*.

Canon Richard Rutt worked as missionary in Korea for 20 years. He is now attached to St Mary Immaculate, Falmouth, Cornwall. (Honorary *D.Litt. of the Confucian University, Seoul.* Joint author with Keith Pratt of Korea: *a Historical and Cultural Dictionary,* London 1999.)

## LAND OF MORNING CALM

Korea in the late 18th century was a land of peace and prosperity. There were poor people in plenty, but the harvests were generally good, there was no trouble from abroad, and the King maintained a benevolent rule that kept the court free of the bloody strife to which it was so liable.

The country was beautiful. Even in the broadest of rice-growing plains, the horizon was lined with blue peaks: distant mountains covered with luxuriant forest trees, among which Siberian tigers roamed. In spring apricot and peach blossom canopied the villages, while the hills were veiled with bright purple azaleas. High summer brought bright green foliage, autumn a rich medley of gold, scarlet and purple. In winter the bald rocks and dark pines were draped in frost and snow. Bamboo delighted poets at all times of the year.

The common people's houses, both in the cities and in the villages that nestled on the sunny slopes of the hills, were built of cob and stone with mushroom-shaped roofs of barley thatch. The houses of the gentry were more elaborate, built of wood with grey tiled roofs turning up at the eaves in Chinese style, with windows of white paper stretched on delicate wooden lattices; but without upper storeys. Similar graceful roofs covered Confucian temples near the towns, and Buddhist temples hidden in the deep mountain valleys. Nearly every beauty spot had its kiosk or pavilion, where in spring and autumn local men would hold picnics at which they all composed Chinese poems.

## A Chinese culture

Every educated man could turn out verses in Chinese rhyme and metre. Education was indeed restricted to mastering the classical Chinese language - pronounced in a Korean fashion - in order to read Chinese literature and Chinese history. All serious books and papers were written in Chinese, and Korean personal names were modelled on Chinese names: surname first, given name afterward, two or three syllables in all. As in China, there were very few surnames, and married women retained their maiden names.

The king was theoretically a vassal of the Chinese Emperor and sent tribute to Beijing every year. Apart from this annual embassy and a few tightly controlled annual markets at border towns, the country had no relations with foreigners. Like China and Japan, Korea was a closed land, allowing neither foreigners in nor its own people out.

Yet the Koreans were a distinctive non-Chinese race with their own language, distantly related to Manchu and other north-east Asian languages. In the 15th century a gifted king had created an alphabet that all but the most underprivileged knew, but only women and labourers

used very much. Chinese was the only writing for men -
save that they too enjoyed the popular novels and songs
that could be written only in Korean.

## Confucianism

With Chinese writing came Confucianism, which provided
Korea's whole philosophy, morals, manners and politics.
Confucius himself was a Chinese sage who flourished at
the beginning of the 5th century BC and taught a 'way'
based on personal goodness, mutual forbearance, reverence
for ancestors and respect for seniors. Confucian temples
were simply halls for honouring ancestors and great sages.
There were no priests or monks: the head of the family or
community officiated at ancestral sacrifices, and there was
no other form of worship, though there were meetings for
instruction of the young and for discussion of principles.
There was a concept of Heaven, which meant both the sky
and a vaguely defined universal deity. Some scholars, both
oriental and Western, have thought that this Heaven was
another name for God, but the records of the 19th-century
martyrs' trials show that this was not the opinion of most
Koreans at that time.

The state was carefully constructed on a Confucian pattern. The king's power was absolute, and since there was
no parliament, there could be no political parties. There
was, however, an unwieldy bureaucracy that provided the
only career possible for a gentleman. Financial corruption

and factional strife were endemic. One group would accuse another of treason or of Confucian heresy, and when the accusation was upheld, the losers were banished to remote corners of the country or barbarously executed. One of the reasons for 18th-century prosperity was the success of a strong king in putting an end to most of these bloodbaths.

## Buddhists and shamans

The heart of Confucian morality was the family. It was a moral duty to marry and have children - celibacy was very wrong in Confucian eyes. Family ancestral sacrifices were the core of Confucian religious practice, and were seen as vital for the unity of the nation. The ceremonies were stately and solemn, strictly non-emotional. They were important for bonding men in both local and national society; but women were excluded. Even had they not been excluded, they found little comfort in the stark rituals. Buddhism, on the other hand, had many prayers, rosaries and ceremonies with incense and lights, which were all more appealing to women. In the Middle Ages it had been the state religion, but the power and politicking of monks had been so abused that since the 16th century no Buddhist temples or monasteries had been allowed in urban areas. The relatively small numbers of monks and nuns withdrew to the mountains, where women of all social classes flocked for picnic and pilgrimage.

There was also a third religious strand: shamanism. Every village would have at least one shaman, usually a woman, a medium who would call up spirits in nightlong ceremonies in clients' homes. The noise of her gongs, songs and dances went on from dusk to dawn. This was a primitive faith with no formalised doctrine, but with a strong hold on the people.

As for Christianity, well-read men had sometimes heard of it. Since the Churches of the Reformation had not yet begun missions in East Asia, for Koreans 'Christian' meant 'Catholic'. They knew there were some Christians in China; but Christianity had been virtually extinguished in Japan, and was kept out of Korea because of respect for Confucius.

## Science and democracy

Korea's unified society, apparently so contented and stable, had in-built flaws, of which none was more keenly felt than the rigid class structure. The educated gentry enjoyed everything that was good in life. They had the privileges of an aristocracy and used their position to extort all they could from the labourers and the poor, who survived at subsistence level. Outdoor folk plays gave vent to their sense of injustice, and the gentry themselves wrote satirical poems about it, but the social system seemed indestructible. Illegitimate sons were most likely to nurse discontent, because the social class of a gentleman's son was determined by the rank of his

mother. While the sons of a rich man's wife would be gentlemen, their half-brothers, born to his concubines, would be
slaves. There were many such illegitimate men, highly con-
scious of injustices of all kinds, and from time to time they
raised rebellions. Thoughtful people realised that the class
system needed to be changed.

Intellectual change was coming too. At the beginning
of the 17th century, western scientific ideas had begun to
interest the Chinese, not least because of the mathematical
and astronomical skills of the French Jesuit mission in
Beijing. Western ideas began to enter Korea when
Chinese books, some of them Christian, were brought
back in the baggage of men who had been with the annual
embassy to Beijing at the winter solstice. Not all Koreans
were impressed; but many became interested in the new
mathematics, better agricultural methods, novel building
techniques and developments in machinery. In a society
that had always treasured the ancient above all, some of
the younger scholars started valuing what was new. There
was no organised movement, but 20th-century historians
named the new wave 'practical learning'.

## A Church founded without missionaries

One of these young intellectuals was 30-year-old Yi Pyök.
He was intrigued by what he read in books from China
that were circulating among his friends. He discovered
that the God of the Christians loved all men equally. This

very reasonable doctrine might lead to changes in social justice. Perhaps he overestimated the stress placed on this point by the Catholic Church of that period, but it led him to further study of the Christian religion, and in 1777 he gathered a few friends of his own age for group study. Such quasi-retreat seminars were typical of the time. They met in a small Buddhist monastery south of the River Han near Seoul, auspiciously named Ch'ŏnjin-sa 'Hermitage of Heavenly Truth'. Politically they were all connected with an old faction that was now in the political wilderness and had no influence at court. Among them were two brothers, Chŏng Yakchong and Chŏng Yagyong. Yagyong was eventually to be recognised under his pen name, Tasan, as the greatest thinker of the day.

They needed more books from China. One of the group, 28-year-old Yi Sŭnghun, a relative of Yi Pyŏk and brother-in-law of the Chŏng brothers, had so far spent a quiet life studying at home; but in 1784 his father was sent as envoy on the annual winter embassy to China. Sŭnghun was thus able to gain a place in the great caravan that made its way over the northern mountains and across the Manchurian plain to Beijing. Members of the embassy always had plenty of time for sightseeing in the capital, and Sŭnghun contrived to visit the French missionaries. The Catholic mission was now in the hands of the Lazarists (the Company of the Mission, also called Vincentians) under the Portuguese Bishop Alexandre de

Gouvea. Sünghun contacted an ex-Jesuit, Fr Jean Grammont, who had stayed in the city after the Jesuit Order was suppressed by the Pope a year earlier. He gave the young Korean some books, crucifixes and other objects, and baptised him with the name of Peter before he returned to Korea at the beginning of 1785.

Yi Pyök and his friends were fascinated by what they now read. Within twelve months they set up a secret church in Seoul at the house of Kim Pömu, one of the royal inter-preters of contemporary Chinese, who was a member of the Hermitage group. (The site of his house is now part of the Catholic cathedral compound in Seoul.) Peter Yi (Sünghun) began baptising them, beginning with Francis Xavier Kwön, a man of about 50. Yi Pyök became Peter, Kim Pömu Thomas, and Chöng Yakchong Augustine. Since Korea knew nothing of a seven-day week, they kept the 7th, 14th, 21st and 28th of each Chinese lunar month as Sunday.

By 1787 they realised a Church needed clergy. Choosing Francis Xavier Kwön as bishop, they also chose a few as priests and began to celebrate mass, confession and confirmation. A few months later they began to have doubts and suspended these ministries until they could consult Bishop de Gouvea through a friend on the annual Beijing embassy. The bishop's reply came in 1790. They had to dismantle their makeshift and invalid priesthood. They must also renounce all Confucian rites. The bishop promised to send them a real priest as soon as he could.

## THE FIRST MARTYRS

Persecution began when they were discovered at prayer in Thomas Kim's house. This socially aberrant behaviour led to them all being questioned. The names of the gentlemen were not published, but, as an interpreter, Thomas was not a gentleman. He belonged to the so-called 'middle' or professional class that included doctors, architects, artists, astronomers and others. He was questioned under torture, found guilty of impiety to the state and banished to Tanyang in the central mountains. On the way there he died in the city of Wŏnju from the injuries he had received during his interrogation. Today he is regarded as the first martyr of the new Church.

A young man named Yun, whose home was in the far south-west of the country and who was in Seoul successfully working his way through the state examination process, had joined the group at Thomas Kim's house in 1784. He was baptised as Paul. In 1789 he joined the embassy to Beijing and while he was there received the sacrament of confirmation from Bishop de Gouvea. On returning home he destroyed the ancestral tablets in the family's Confucian shrine, and when his mother died in 1791 he had her buried without Confucian rites. He and an elder cousin named James Kwŏn were arrested for this impiety that threatened the whole structure of the nation.

They were taken to the provincial capital at Chönju and beheaded. At least eight other men were martyred in the south-western regions before 1799. To become a Christian was dangerous.

Defections were to be expected. Yi Pyök, Chöng Yagyong, Francis Xavier Kwön and even the first baptised, Peter Yi, were among those who withdrew, persuaded by their families. Many Korean Catholics today are convinced that some of them returned later, but we can be sure of Peter Yi only. He was destined for martyrdom.

### A woman in charge

Bishop de Gouvea did not forget his promise. He despatched a priest in 1791, a Fr Wu; but Fr Wu was unable to enter Korea and returned to Beijing, where he died two years later. Then in winter 1794 Fr Zhou Wenmo, baptised James, managed to reach Seoul. He celebrated mass for the first time at Easter 1795. Alexander Hwang, a brilliant young son-in-law of the Chöng family, served as his interpreter and Korean tutor. As a Chinese in Korean dress, Zhou would attract no attention, but when he spoke his accent would betray him as a foreigner and the fact that he was a priest would have led to his arrest. For the next seven years he worked secretly among the 4,000 or so Christians in the capital and surrounding countryside, making his base in the house, or rather in the woodshed, of a woman called Columba Kang. He made her a catechist.

The Korean word for catechist literally means 'leader of the congregation' and catechists had a broad pastoral role in teaching, organising, guiding and encouraging the faithful. Columba became the most powerful member of the Church, because she controlled access to Fr Zhou, and she alone always knew where he was.

She had become a Christian in her home region in the Naep'o district south of Seoul, near the west coast, one of the first districts to be evangelised and one that produced more martyrs than any other. Her husband divorced her because of her Christian faith and she moved to Seoul with her mother-in-law, daughter and stepson, all Christians. She had independent means and partly financed Fr Zhou's journey from China. As catechist, she recruited and trained women workers and generally over-saw the Christian women. She converted two royal princesses: Princess Song, a sister-in-law of the King, and Princess Song's daughter-in-law, Princess Sin. Astute and capable, Columba kept Fr Zhou's presence secret until 1801, when he was arrested. She and four of her helpers were arrested too and fiercely tortured.

Fr Zhou was executed by the elaborate and sickening ritual of 'decapitation and display'. The two princesses were convicted of having dealings with a foreign male, adopting evil teachings and leaving the palace precincts. They too were executed. Columba was beheaded at the West Gate prison on 3 July. She has not yet been beatified, because the documentation is incomplete, but the Korean Church is now forwarding her cause, together with the causes of 16 other martyrs. Even though more Korean women than men have been canonised, the canonisation of Columba Kang would bring more attention to the powerful role of women in the story of Korea's martyrs. In periods of persecution women are always vital to the strength of the Church: they train their sons and daughters to be ready for martyrdom. Columba did more. She was for seven crucial years the chief organiser of the Church.

## Arrest and torture

The martyrs were treated as ordinary malefactors. They were arrested by the police, who bound them with red cord and took them to the Police Prison, often called in English the Thieves' Prison. This appalling place was an unpaved yard - usually mud or dust - surrounded by sheds with fronts of stout wooden bars, built against the walls. Men and women were separated, but otherwise all prisoners were packed in together, with no protection against freezing cold in winter or scorching heat in summer. Prisoners were allowed into the central open space during daylight hours. At night they were forced into the sheds, where they usually had no room to stretch or to lie down. Once the doors were closed they were not opened until dawn for any purpose at all. There was no sanitation. Disease was rife. Prisoners were given a pitifully small

ration of boiled millet twice a day, though some were
able to buy or bribe extra food. Others ate foul straw and
lice. It was said that some Christians who bore tortures
with fortitude collapsed and apostatised under the strain
of prison conditions. Others often claimed that imprisonment was harder to bear than torture.

After interrogators had compiled the evidence against
the prisoners under the police procedure, which might
take many days, those who were not released were sent to
the Criminal Court Prison. This was similar to the Police
Prison, though sometimes less crowded.

Interrogations were normally accompanied by torture.
Merciless beating was administered with a variety of pad-
dles, besoms, scourges, rods and wands, each inflicting its
own peculiar kind of pain. Savage beating caused blood-
shed and there are accounts of martyrs whose flesh fell off
in shreds, even of bones being exposed. Wooden blocks
and ropes were employed to bend leg and arm bones, even
to break them and dislocate joints. Pointed bamboo rods
might be stuck into the victim's flesh. In another torture a
cord was passed under the victim's thighs, crossed over
the front and then held taut by a man on either side who
applied a sawing motion that cut through the flesh like a
wire cheese-cutter, right through to the bone. Such tortures would be repeated over many days, even weeks. Few
martyrs, if any, escaped being tortured again when they
were brought to the execution ground.

## Execution

Some executions were carried out by strangling. This was usually done in the Police Prison. The prisoner was placed between two posts. The rope was passed round his neck, the ends crossed at the front. Each end was then wound round one of the posts and drawn tight by an executioner. Most of the martyrs were, however, beheaded at an execution ground outside the Little West Gate of the city. The condemned person was tied by hands and hair to a large cross erected on a bull-cart, and deliberately driven by a rocky and steep road, calculated to make the journey as painful as possible. At the site there was a block at which the victim was made to kneel. The head was cut off with a huge sword. Several blows were needed to finish the work. (During the decapitation of St John Pak the executioner actually withdrew after striking a few blows in order to whet his blade. Then he returned and finished severing the head.)

When the authorities wanted to make the public more widely aware of an execution, it was not performed at one of the relatively small execution grounds, but at a place where a far larger number of spectators could be assembled. At Seoul that usually meant the broad sands of the Han River, near the big flat island of Yöüido and the army training camp, a mile or so further west than the regular execution ground.

The procedure was called 'displaying the head before the military camp'. It was a military function, with one of the commandants of the capital garrison in attendance at the head of a hundred or so soldiers. A tall stake was erected on the sands for each of the condemned. The man was brought to the place, bound in a rough wooden chair, carried by two soldiers with an escort. On arrival he was stripped to his floppy white trousers, and his topknot unravelled (Buddhist monks alone did not wear top-knots). An arrow was thrust downwards though the top and lobe of each of his ears. His face was dashed with water and lime, his hands tied in front of his chest. Two poles were put under the rope binding his wrists and one pole pushed under each armpit. Two men, one in front and one behind, took the ends of these poles, lifted the victim and carried him three times round the arena, to the execration and insults of the crowd. A soldier attached a banner to the top of the stake, inscribed with the crime in Chinese, while another read out the sentence. The man was then ordered to kneel back to the stake. His hair was gathered in a bunch and tied to the stake to stretch his neck so that his head was ready for severing. A small troop of soldiers then performed a slow dance round the stake, chanting and brandishing heavy sabres, with which they struck his neck. Several blows were needed to sever it. As the head rolled off, another soldier picked it up and presented it on a tray to the presiding commandant. The head was then displayed on a stake, as a warning to the public, and left there for three days. It was forbidden that anyone should touch the corpses. This ritual execution was used for all foreign missionaries and for other Christians to whom the authorities wanted to draw attention.

## 1801, The Year of the White Cock

Three hundred Christians were executed that year in an outburst of violence that has gone down in history as the 'Persecution of the White Cock Year', because the Koreans numbered their years according to the twelve Chinese 'zodiacal' animals. Although there had been martyrdoms nearly every year since 1791, there was no policy of seeking out Christians until the Year of the White Cock, 1801, when a change of policy followed the accession to the throne in 1800 of a ten-year-old boy.

When a child became king, the senior Queen Dowager acted as regent until he was of an age to rule for himself. Since there were no other royal families in Asia for the kings to marry into, they had to marry women of their own country, which inevitably gave political power to the families from which the queens came. In 1800 the Queen Dowager was from a family in the conservative tradition, which disapproved of Christians because they were favoured by those who followed the 'practical learning' vogue. Christianity was already being called 'Western teaching'. She ordered that Catholics should be sought out, and executed if they would not apostatise.

Things were made worse by the incident of the 'silk letter'. During the year Fr Zhou's 25-year-old tutor, Alexander Hwang, wrote a letter on a roll of silk to the Bishop of Beijing, asking for the Pope to send military assistance to the Korean Christians. The letter (now in the Vatican) was intercepted, Hwang was executed, and there was further reason for the government to attack Christians.

Peter Yi - the man who had first brought Christian books to the scholars at the Hermitage of Heavenly Truth 27 years before, but apostatised - returned to the faith and was among those martyred in the Year of the White Cock. So was Augustine Chöng.

### Thirty-five years waiting for a priest

For its first ten years (1784-1794) the Korean Church had no sacrament but baptism. Now again it had no priest. This time it would have to wait for thirty-five years. Soon the young king married a woman from the Andong Kim family, which was sympathetic to the liberalising intellectuals. Persecution eased, but the frontiers remained tightly closed. There were probably 7,000 or 8,000 Christians throughout the country, mostly in Seoul and the south-western provinces, drawn almost entirely from the gentry and professional classes.

A natural leader appeared among them: Peter Yi's cousin, Paul Chöng Hasang, son of the martyred

Augustine Chöng. Paul's brother also was martyred in 1801. His mother and sisters, though reduced to poverty, brought him up as a devoted Christian and provided him with an excellent home education. At the age of 20 he got a post as a servant on the annual embassy to Beijing. He was able to do this again on nine subsequent occasions, and thus to maintain contact with Bishop de Gouvea. In spite of his youth, he was appointed catechist and effectively became the lay pastor of all the Christians in the country. He persisted in efforts to get another priest from China, and very nearly succeeded with a Fr Shen in 1826, but that plan came to nothing. Korea still had to wait for a priest.

In 1823 Paul was introduced to a man four years his senior named Yu, a remarkable scholar and famous book-collector. One day Yu had noticed that the paper used to line a drawer in his furniture had scraps of philosophy printed on it. Intrigued, he succeeded in stripping all the fragments from the cabinetwork and found he had part of a treatise on the true meaning of God, written by Mateo Ricci, the greatest of the China Jesuits. In his attempts to find someone who would explain more about Ricci's ideas, Yu met Paul Chöng. They became firm friends. Yu held a senior post in the royal interpreters' bureau and frequently went on the annual mission to Beijing. Paul found a place as a servant on the embassy in 1824 and they both went to see Bishop de Gouvea. While they were there, Yu was baptised, taking the name of Augustine.

Soon his authority in the Korean Church was less only than that of Paul Chöng.

On one of these Beijing journeys Paul and Augustine got to know a servant in his twenties named Cho, an able man with an unusual spiritual history. For a while he had been a Buddhist monk. Paul and Augustine recognised his qualities and encouraged him to become a Christian. He was baptised and confirmed in Beijing, with the name of Charles. On return to Korea he became a trusted helper, willing to undertake difficult and dangerous tasks.

The instruction of new Christians continued with zeal. Every year saw more manuals and prayerbooks arriving from China, including stories of saints. Saints' names were always given at baptism, in Chinese form and with a seeming preference for the names of martyrs - Lucy, Agnes, Sebastian, Protase and the like. Korean Christians knew they might need the help and example of earlier Christian martyrs.

In 1825 Paul and Augustine, with some others, sent an earnest letter for help to Pope Leo XII. It was received two years later, but nothing came of it until Pope Gregory XVI, as part of his revival of world missions (he established some 70 new dioceses and vicariates), created the Korean Vicariate Apostolic in 1831. This was the first step towards creating a Korean diocese.

## FRENCH MISSIONARIES

The new vicariate was entrusted to the Paris Foreign
Missions Society, which had been working in east and
south-east Asia for two centuries. Barthélemy Bruguière,
a priest who had been two years in Bangkok, was
appointed Vicar Apostolic and ordained bishop. He set
out for Korea overland from Thailand in 1831. A young
priest called Jacques Chastan, recently arrived at Penang
in Malaya, was detailed to join him. Then Fr Pierre
Maubant, who was working in Sichuan (western China),
volunteered to join the Bishop as he passed through
Sichuan on his way to Korea.

Before any of them could get there, however, a
Chinese priest named Pacifico Yu, who was studying in
the Chinese College at Naples, volunteered to work in the
new vicariate. Paul Chöng, Augustine Yu and another of
the gentry class, Sebastian Nam, helped him to enter the
country in 1833. Sebastian lived with Fr Pacifico in Seoul
and took care of him.

Meanwhile Bishop Bruguière and Fr Maubant travelled the length of China by separate routes. They met in
Manchuria and stayed in a tiny Christian village they
thought was a suitable place from which to attempt crossing the Korean border. While waiting there the bishop fell
ill and died on 20 October 1835, broken by the exertions

of the journey. He was 43 years old. Fr Maubant, a strong man in his twenties, went on alone. No European could get through the frontier guardposts. The only way he could enter Korea was to wait till the depth of winter and struggle over the River Yalu when it was frozen. Helped and guided by Paul Chöng, Fr Maubant crossed the ice at night in January 1836.

He had to disguise himself as a mourner, because mourners wore huge umbrella-like straw hats that hid their faces and his brown beard would show he was not a Korean. Travelling on foot in severe winter weather, usually at night and in constant risk of discovery, he took 15 days to reach Seoul, where he was greeted by Fr Pacifico, Sebastian Nam and others. Immediately he was swamped with pastoral work, travelling among the scattered flock in the two central provinces, often accompanied by Charles Cho, he who had once been a Buddhist monk but now became the Frenchman's guide and interpreter. People who had not been able to make their confessions for thirty-five years could do so at last. Some made their confessions in written Chinese, others had to use interpreters. On Holy Saturday they celebrated the Vigil of Easter in the cramped space of an ordinary Korean house - a clandestine liturgy lasting five hours.

Fr Maubant's most important achievement was the selection of three teenage boys to become seminarians: Francis-Xavier Kim, Andrew Kim and Thomas Ch'oe.

Accompanied by Fr Pacifico (who never returned), they were smuggled out of Korea in 1836 and sent to the Paris Society's seminary at Macao. Paul Chŏng, Augustine Yu and Sebastian Nam saw them out of the country.

The other French priest, Jacques Chastan, had reached the northern frontier in 1833. He was the same age as Maubant. He had come by sea routes from Penang to Macao, thence to Fujian, and finally by a fishermen's boat to Manchuria. Though he came within sight of the mountains of Korea, he could find no way to cross the frontier. He therefore withdrew and worked for about two years in Shandong until he could get a message to Fr Maubant, who was by then in Seoul. Fr Maubant arranged for couriers to meet and help him; but they then had to wait until the Yalu froze. Fr Chastan crossed the ice on the last day of the year 1836, arriving in Seoul in January 1837.

During the summer both priests managed to give a few weeks to language study, though they never dared stay long in one place. They had to acclimatise themselves to rough food, especially the standard meal of turnip pickled in brine, served with rice and thin soup. Dried persimmon fruit served them as iron rations, for they were constantly travelling on foot, sleeping by day, saying mass and doing pastoral work at night. Fr Maubant fell ill. Fr Chastan rushed to see him in Seoul and gave him the last rites. Miraculously, he recovered, and after three months rest returned to the punishing work that had brought him

low. They had some 6,000 Christians to look after.
During 1837 they heard over 2,000 confessions and baptised 1,237 new Christians.

## A pastoral bishop

Communications with Europe were very slow. At length
Laurent Imbert, a priest of the Paris Missions who had
been working in Sichuan, western China, since 1820, and
knew Pierre Maubant, was appointed bishop for Korea,
and ordained in May 1837. By November he had arrived
at Mukden (now Shenyang) in Manchuria. In mid-
December, he crossed the frozen Yalu and on New Year's
Day 1838 he met Fr Maubant in Seoul. Fr Chastan was
away in the south, and did not meet the bishop until May.

Between the bishop's arrival and November 1837,
2,000 were baptised. By the end of the year there were
9,000 Korean Christians. Imbert soon recognised that
Paul Chöng would make a good priest. He even went so
far as to start teaching him some Latin and a little the-
ology. In spite of the enormous difficulties, there were
gleams of hope.

The bishop's life scarcely differed from that of his
priests. He rose at 2.30 a.m. At 3.30 he began baptising,
confessing, confirming, celebrating mass and caring for the
Christians, who rarely dared to be seen coming and going
in daylight. He suffered from hunger, because he often
could not eat until his pastoral work was finished for the

day. He went to sleep at 9 in the evening. 'A life so hard', he wrote, 'we hardly fear the sword-blow that must end it'.

## 1839, The Year of the Yellow Pig

The premonition was apt. A new king had come to the throne in 1834, one whose in-laws were opposed to what they called 'western learning' - meaning Christianity. Christians had to be more careful, and by the time the bishop arrived, persecution was intensifying. Peter Yi, a catechist, had been imprisoned for four years but not executed. He died on 25 November 1838 in the Criminal Court Prison. His sister Agatha had been arrested in February 1836 and was still held in prison. Pressure on Christians increased during spring and summer 1839, the Year of the Yellow Pig. A stern new decree against Christianity was published in April.

We have records of some 140 martyrs during the whole year, in Seoul and several southern provincial cities, but this can be only part of the whole story. Dispossessed Christians were taking refuge in the further parts of the country. Already some of them were becoming potters, because makers of earthenware traditionally travelled from place to place in search of suitable clay, setting up earth kilns in waste places and moving on when they had exhausted local clay deposits. Itinerant potters were to remain a feature of the Korean Catholic Church for two hundred years.

In mid-May Protase Chöng, a man of 41, was arrested and questioned by a kindly magistrate who persuaded him to deny his faith. Protase went home, but could not rest. A few days later he presented himself to the police, demanding to be re-arrested. They refused to take him seriously. He redoubled his demand. Finally they beat him severely and threw him into prison, where, a few hours later, he died during the night.

### Three men and six women, 24 May 1839

On 24 May Agatha Yi was beheaded with eight others, including the catechist Augustine Yi, on an execution ground outside the Little West Gate of Seoul. The police had found a silver mitre (whose workmanship astounded them), a chasuble and a Latin prayerbook in the catechist's house. This discovery strengthened the government's determination to find the illegal foreign entrants.

Most of that day's martyrs were of the gentry class. Lucy Pak had rich relations in the royal palace. Damian Nam, however, declared that he would be happy to enter heaven with no other rank than 'Damian Nam of the Scapular Confraternity'. Anna Pak was devoted to the Five Wounds of Christ. Agatha Kim was such a simple soul that she could only repeat the names of Jesus and Mary. She was baptised in prison. The others were Magdalene Kim, Barbara Han and Peter Kwön, whose beatific smile was said to have survived on his severed head.

A day or two later there were three deaths in the Police Prison. One of these was 14-year-old Barbara Yi. The others were Barbara Kim and Joseph Chang the herbalist.

## One man and seven women, 20 July 1839

Executions continued throughout the summer. The next canonised names are those of a man and seven women beheaded on 20 July. The man was John Yi, brother of Augustine Yi, martyred in May. John had been baptised in Peking when he was there as a member of the annual embassy.

The eldest woman was Rosa Kim, a convert widow in her mid-fifties, who calmly murmured the names of Jesus and Mary as she was arrested. Anna Kim was a few years younger. Maria Wön was only 20. She had been orphaned at 9 and was brought up as, Christian. She was determined to stay a virgin. For that reason she dressed her hair like a married woman's and earned a living by needlework. When neighbours delated her to the police, she tried to run away but failed - she had some difficulty in coming to terms with her situation. Magdalene Yi had never seen Seoul before she left her pagan father's house in the countryside to find a Christian family to live with in Seoul. She followed her father to Seoul without his knowledge, and by leaving bloodstained shreds of her clothing in the woods on the way, successfully persuaded her family that a tiger had killed her. Her father soon learned the truth, but forgave her. Lucy Kim had a fine head of hair, which she sold in prison in order to buy thin soup for other starving prisoners. She had joined with Theresa Yi, Martha Kim and Lucy Kim in a pact to surrender themselves to the authorities and seek martyrdom. The judges gave them extra tortures to punish their presumption.

Agnes Kim also died that day. She was the younger sister of Columba Kim, a remarkable woman who was to die a fortnight later.

### The maker of straw shoes

On 3 September another man and five women were beheaded outside the Little West Gate. The man was John Pak, a maker of straw shoes who had often said he needed to die a martyr in order to atone for his sins, striking his shin with the mallet of his trade as he said it. He had sent his wife away to stay with relations the night before he was arrested.

The eldest of the women was Maria Pak, whose sister Lucy had died on 24 May. Barbara Kwön and Maria Yi, wife of Damian Nam, had each made her house a mass-centre for Bishop Imbert. Barbara Yi had insisted on marrying a Christian, and had put off a pagan suitor by staying abed for three years pretending to be unable to walk. She had then married a Christian, but he had died after only two years. Her sister Magdalene and her aunt

Theresa had been beheaded on 20 July, her young niece, also called Barbara Yi, had died in prison at the end of May; and she left her mother Magdalene Hö in jail, waiting for martyrdom.

## Father of a priest

A week later, on 12 September, Francis Ch'oe, aged only 34, father of the lad Thomas who had been sent to the seminary in Macao with two other boys in 1836, died in prison. Francis had been baptised when young. He had a fiery temperament, which he succeeded in controlling, so that the impression he left on others was one of generosity and gentleness. When he realised persecution was growing, he hid his pious medals and other devotional objects, but did nothing to hide his Christian books. He said the images must be protected against sacrilege, but the books were his manuals of strategy in the coming battle.

When police came to his home in the country to fetch him, he entertained them overnight - and gave new clothes to one of them whose clothes were threadbare. Then he persuaded a group of nearly forty Christians to go to prison with him, saying it would be better to die by the sword in Seoul than to starve in the country - for there was a famine that year. Only three of the forty stayed to the end. When asked to renounce his Christian faith, Francis replied that if asked to live without eating, he would try, though it would be very difficult; but it was impossible for him to pretend not to believe in God. At one point he was asked to put on the bishop's vestments. He refused, and they were put on another prisoner. Francis straightway prostrated himself before the man. When asked whom he was reverencing, he replied, 'The crucifix'. The questioner raised his hand to strike Francis; then thought better of it.

The officers goaded a repulsive thief to insult and pester him, even to opening and hurting the sores from his beatings. Francis bore everything with such resignation that the thief exclaimed, 'He really is a Christian. You other Christians! Do as he does!'

On 11 September he was beaten with 50 blows - having been beaten every second day since the beginning of August. The next day he died in prison, disappointed that God had not allowed him to shed his blood, but accepting the Divine Will.

### The good shepherd gives up his life for the sheep

So many of his flock were being imprisoned, tortured and executed that Bishop Imbert wondered whether he and the two priests should try to leave the country, in order to save the laity. The three Frenchmen met near Suwŏn, but, deciding that any plan to leave Korea would be impracticable, they separated on 3 July and went into hiding.

On 10 August a new Christian named Andrew Chŏng came to the bishop in the middle of the night, saying a messenger had come from Seoul, where the government had changed its mind and would now treat him with due honour. Imbert realised at once that his hiding place had been betrayed. He wrote straightway to his two priests, then went to meet the 'messenger' in a nearby village. The messenger turned out to be an apostate called Kim Yösang. The bishop went with him to Seoul. There he was soon bound with the red cord of arrest, and taken for questioning with the usual tortures. He had persuaded the police to allow Andrew Chöng return to his own home.

Anxious now to find the two priests, the police deceived two more Christians, one of whom went along with the ruse so far as to meet the bishop, from whom he was able to take a note for Fr Maubant and Fr Chastan, written in Latin. The note said: 'In extreme circumstances the good shepherd gives his life for the sheep, so if you have not already left, come with the officer Son Kyejong, but do not let any of the Christians follow you. Imbert, Bishop of Capsa.' (Capsa was his titular see, because Korea was not yet a diocese.)

The letter soon reached Fr Maubant, who sent it on to Fr Chastan and at the same time wrote to Son, telling him that Fr Chastan was away, but they would both arrive in about ten days. Jacques Chastan received the message on 1 September. He at once sat down and wrote a farewell letter to his family in France, giving thanks to God for calling him to be a martyr. When the two met,

near the town of Hongju, they both wrote further letters
on 6 September, to the Maubant family, to the Roman
Propaganda and to the Paris Foreign Missions Society.
They reported to Cardinal Fransoni of the Propaganda
that the mission had about 10,000 Christians. They also
reported 1,200 baptisms, 2,500 confirmations, 4,500 confessions, 4,000 communions, 150 marriages, 60 anoint-
ings of the dying, and 600 catechumens under instruction. For three men this was a huge accomplishment,
especially when the necessary travelling and the language difficulties are taken into account. They both then
wrote letters to their Christians, exhorting them particularly to ensure that Christians married Christians.

From Hongju they were taken on ponies to Seoul. On
12 September they were in Seoul with their bishop, all
three being interrogated by the Criminal Court. They were
beaten on the 15th and 16th and again on the 19th. They
were finally sentenced late on the 21st, and executed on
the sands by the Han that evening. The whole ritual of
military decapitation with display of the heads was gone
through. When Fr Chastan received the first sword blow it
fell on his shoulder and he started up, but immediately fell
back on his knees. Otherwise they remained still till they
died. Not until three weeks later were Christians able to
disinter the three bodies surreptitiously and take them
away. Many decades later they were enshrined in the crypt
of Seoul cathedral.

Late in the afternoon of the next day Paul Chöng and his fellow-worker Augustine Yu were beheaded outside the Little West Gate.

So the leadership of the infant Church was destroyed in two days. Bishop Imbert, realising that this would happen, had committed the Church to the care Charles Hyön, a gifted catechist of the professional class.

## Strong women

Four days after Paul and Augustine were killed, nine other Christians were martyred outside the Little West Gate on 26 September. The six women among them had been under arrest for many weeks - Magdalene Pak for six months. She and Agatha Chön had connections with the palace, where she had lived and worked. Perpetua Hong had been in prison for over four months, Columba Kim since June and Julietta Kim since July. Magdalene Hö was the mother of Barbara Yi and Magdalene Yi, who had been beheaded on 20 July and 2 September.

The life of women, especially those of the gentry class, was severely circumscribed. They rarely travelled, indeed rarely left the house and were not allowed in the streets in daylight. Most of them could not read Chinese characters. They were conventionally regarded as unintelligent. The truth was very different. In spite of their manner of life, women were often of strong character, perceptive, and influential in the lives of the men.

Their steadfastness is illustrated by their response to torture. It was allied to a meekness and dignity that were in themselves virtues for Confucians too. Most of these women had been looking forward to martyrdom, some for many years. Perpetua Hong had long said she wanted 'to wear the red dress (of martyrdom)'. When they came to interrogation they surprised the questioners by the cogency of their arguments for believing in God and Christ.

Columba Kim made a great impression by her poise and lack of fear. She had been imprisoned with her sister Agnes, who had been beheaded three weeks earlier. They were aged 26 and 23. Their questioners were so exasperated by their constancy that the women had been stripped of all their clothing and put into a men's section of the Police Prison, with a suggestion that the ruffians already there were welcome to treat the women as they liked. After two days they were given back their clothes and returned, untouched, to the women's prison. When they were next under torture Columba complained about this incident with calm dignity. She said she would not complain about treatment that was legal, but she and her sister had been treated illegally. The court was appalled and sent a report to higher authority. Some of the prison staff were punished with severe bastinado.

Columba could be satirical too, as she was in describing the nonsense involved in believing that the souls of the dead would come and enjoy the meal prepared for them in the

Confucian ancestral sacrifice ritual. She won admiration for her intelligence and courage, but these virtues could not spare her; nor would she have wished that they might.

Also in September another Lucy Kim, 70 years old and generally known as 'the hunchback', died in prison.

## Three male martyrs and three more women

On 26 September three more men were executed with the six women: Charles Cho, Sebastian Nam and Ignatius Kim. They represented the second level of leadership in the Church

Charles Cho and Sebastian Nam had been among those who went on the embassies to Beijing. Charles, who went every year, had helped to arrange for the foreign priests to enter Korea and had acted as guide for Maubant in his pastoral journeys. On his return from China at the beginning of 1839, he had received a vision of Christ with St Peter and St Paul, which he had interpreted as a promise of martyrdom. When he was taken from the cross on the cart that took him to the execution ground, Charles Cho noticed some of his relations, not Christians, present there in great distress. He gave them an affectionate smile.

Sebastian Nam had been Fr Pacifico's helper and was an experienced leader in the Church. He also was taken through the treachery of a Christian.

Ignatius Kim, whose own father had been martyred in 1814, was father of the boy Andrew Kim who had gone to Macao in 1836 to study for the priesthood. Ignatius broke under torture, but was still condemned to punishment for having let his son go abroad. When he was returned to prison, the others encouraged him to reassert his faith. This he did three times, under increased torture; and so died a martyr.

On the last night of the month two more women died in prison, both of them sick with disease contracted from the conditions under which they were detained: 57-year-old Catherine Yi and her 33-year-old daughter Magdalene Cho. Catherine had been reduced to poverty by her persistence in the faith and earned a meagre living as a seamstress. She realised her ambition of dying a virgin.

### Boy martyr

Augustine Yu's family, of whom only two had accepted their father's faith, was outlawed and banished from the capital. Before then, however, his younger son Peter, aged 13, had become the youngest of the martyrs who would be canonised 150 years later. This remarkable boy had begun to hope for martyrdom long before. After his father was arrested he had gone to the police early in August and urged them to arrest him. They did so and proceeded to question him with torture on 14 occasions. At least once he picked up shreds of his flesh from the ground and threw them defiantly before the judges. To many of the onlookers it seemed that he was happy throughout the five horrific weeks, hoping to be beheaded. In the event he was strangled in the prison on 31 October.

## Paul's mother

Paul Chöng's mother, Cecilia Yu, was 79 years old. The police arrested her on 19 July and subjected her, old as she was, to 230 strokes of the wand in her first 5 interrogations. She wanted to join her beloved Paul in martyrdom, but because of her age the authorities would not behead her. She resigned herself to dying in prison, and lingered on until she fell asleep on 23 November, quietly murmuring the names of Jesus and Mary. Her daughter Elisabeth was still alive in prison for her faith.

## Winter martyrs

On the day Cecilia died, 23 November 1839, the State council issued an even stronger edict against Christianity. On 29 December, seven more martyrs were killed.

Benedicta Hyön was sister to Charles Hyön, the catechist who had become leader of the new generation. Their father had died for the faith in 1801. Magdalene Yi was an impoverished lady of the gentry class who had watched her mother die in prison. Peter Ch'oe, father-in-law of Charles Cho, was a man of the professional class who after a dissolute youth had become a Christian and tamed his wild ways. Magdalene Han was married to a distinguished scholar who had been baptised *in articulo*

*mortis*. Cecilia Yu's daughter and Paul Chŏng's sister,
Elisabeth Chŏng, had always lived in poverty and was
accustomed to earn her pittance by needlework and weav-
ing. She was the fourth member of her family to be executed. Bishop Imbert declared she should have been made
a catechist. As she left the prison on her way to execution, she exhorted those she left behind to pray always for
the poor and for the suffering. Barbara Cho was the wife
of Sebastian Nam, who had died among those killed on
26 September. She was also cousin of Paul Chŏng and
had kept house for Fr Pacifico. Barbara Ko had been a
toddler when her father had been martyred in 1801. She
left her husband Augustine Pak in prison, awaiting his
inevitable death before long.

## Strangulations

January 1840 saw four martyrs strangled in the Police Prison.
On the 9th the two victims were women. Theresa Kim
was an aunt of the boy Andrew Kim who had gone to
Macao to study for the priesthood four years earlier. Her
husband Joseph Son had died in prison for the faith in
1824 in the country town of Haemi. She had provided a
home for Fr Pacifico till he went with the three boys to
China. Later she joined Bishop Imbert's household. She
was strangled after nearly six months' imprisonment.
Agatha Yi, who died the same day aged only 17, had
been imprisoned in April, with her father Augustine

(beheaded in April) and her mother Barbara Kwön (beheaded in September).

Later the same month, the same brutal death put an end to the sufferings of two more men. The first was 35-year-old Andrew Chöng, the naive convert who had fallen into the trap set by the apostate Kim Yösang to capture Bishop Imbert. Andrew had been duped again into betraying some new converts; but he woke to the truth when Kim tried to persuade him to betray Fr Maubant and Fr Chastan. In his distress at that time Andrew spoke of giving himself up to martyrdom. The priests dissuaded him; but he was soon caught and subjected to rigorous tortures. Five months later he was strangled on 23 January 1840.

His companion in martyrdom, Stephen Min, was killed a week later. He was nearly 60, a childless widower, reduced to staying in other peoples' houses, earning a living by hand-copying books. His sufferings climaxed in 40 strokes of the paddle, at every one of which he cried 'A rascal fit only to die!' Yet in those last weeks of misery this rather solemn soul managed to persuade two apostates to repent: Dominic Yi and Cosmas Yö - both of whom were executed before Stephen himself.

### Five men and five women

Ten martyrs died on 31 January and 1 February 1840 - five men and five women.

Paul Hö was a soldier of the city garrison. At first he broke down under the torture, but soon he recovered his courage and was subjected to depraved tests by the guards, who made him eat and drink filth to prove his fidelity to Christ. He died while being tortured by beating with the heavy paddle.

The other nine were beheaded at Tang-Kogae, another place of execution outside the western walls of the city. The five women were all at least acquaintances, if not friends. Maria Yi was sister of Magdalene Yi, beheaded with six others on 29 December. Magdalene Son was the wife of Peter Ch'oe, who had also been martyred on that December day. Barbara Ch'oe was their daughter, whose husband Charles Cho had been martyred in September. Magdalene was another seamstress, and both she and her daughter each arrived in prison with a tiny daughter. Both children were sent away into the care of others.

The fourth woman, Agatha Kwön, was a stranger case. She died at the age of 21 and was the daughter of Magalene Han, who had been beheaded outside the Little West Gate at the end of December. Magdalene's husband had been converted on his deathbed. They had arranged for Agatha to be married at the age of 12. Marriage at this age was more common than not, and the bride and groom were not expected to cohabit until some years later. This bridegroom's family, however, was too poor even to take Agatha to live in their house and she was confided to his relations. When Fr Pacifico arrived in Korea she entered service in his household. He became very fond of her, and approved her wish to break off her marriage and live as a virgin. Their relationship became too close and gave cause for scandal. Fr Maubant talked to her and she became overwhelmed with penitence, claiming that only martyrdom would expiate her sins. Kim Yŏsang, who had betrayed Bishop Imbert, sank further into depravity by trying to persuade her to go off with him, but she was steadfast. She entered the prison with some happiness. The guards were sorry for Agatha and set her free, but she soon returned voluntarily to the prison. Her martyrdom was a singular triumph at the close of a life of frailty and great trials.

The fifth woman was Agatha Yi. She had been married to a eunuch. Bishop Imbert advised that she should leave him, but her mother was too poor to support her. She moved in with Agatha Kwŏn and was arrested with her.

Of the four men, two were brothers aged 39 and 42: Peter and Paul Hong from Sŏsan district in the central province, grandsons and nephews of two martyrs of 1801. Both were catechists and had helped shelter Fr Maubant and Fr Chastan in spring and summer 1839. The dastardly Kim Yŏsang fingered them as he did the bishop and the two priests.

Augustine Pak was 48, a member of the professional class, cultured and kind, but very poor. His wife Barbara

Ko, whose own father had been martyred in 1801, had been beheaded in November. Augustine had been one of the group that arranged for the three Frenchmen to enter the country and Bishop Imbert had made him a catechist. It is recorded that he was insulted and tortured even by other prisoners. The torturers left him unable to use either arms or legs.

The last of the group was John Yi, 31 years old. He was of the gentry class, a widower without children. He had accompanied Fr Maubant on pastoral journeys. During 1839 he had been at pains to offer relief to imprisoned Christians; and he had led the group that secretly removed the bodies of the three French martyrs from the Han River sands at the end of September. Six days before he died he wrote a lengthy letter of advice to his fellow-Christians, trying to strengthen their faith. He advised them particularly to practise the Stations of the Cross frequently and to have recourse to the prayers of the Ever-virgin Mary.

Barbara Ch'oe and Paul Hong could not be executed with the others, because no one could be beheaded on the same day as a close relation. Paul had a brother, and Barbara her mother, among the condemned. Seven of the group were therefore beheaded on 31 January, but these two and John Yi on 1 February.

The list of those canonised for the persecution of the Year of the Yellow Pig ends with Antony Kim strangled on 29 April 1841, after 15 months in prison.

## Rebellions and poor harvests

For the next six years there were few martyrdoms. The royal in-laws were Kims again, favourable to modern learning, and the police stopped searching out Christians. The Church however could not lower its guard. Most Christians were hiding in the countryside, and all had been impoverished. Few remained who belonged to the gentry. Not only had they lost all their priests; they had lost their Korean leaders too. Three men remained who could give some leadership, but they were less gifted than Paul Chöng and his companions: Fr Chastan's servant, Charles Hyön; Fr Maubant's servant, Peter Chöng; and Thomas Yi, a grandson of the very first Korean to be baptised in Beijing, Peter Yi, martyred in 1801.

The state of the whole country was now far from being as prosperous as it had been when Peter Yi collected Christian books in Beijing for the scholars of the Hermitage of Heavenly Truth. Government by the royal in-laws had been corrupt; the kings had lacked charisma; there had been too many poor harvests; and a succession of uprisings, led by illegitimate sons and other malcontents, showed the general malaise of the nation.

The Paris Foreign Missions Society and the Office of Propaganda in Rome appointed John Joseph Ferréol as Vicar Apostolic for Korea. He arrived in Manchuria by sea and reached Shenyang (then called Mukden) in 1840. He was unable to get further for four years. Had Paul

Chŏng still been alive, things might have been different. Christians were still able from time to time to get on the embassies from Seoul to Beijing, but the network had been broken. Ferréol withdrew beyond the Mongolian border and stayed with the little Christian community that had sheltered Bishop Bruguière five years earlier. Not until 1842 was contact established with Charles Hyŏn. The way would soon be open. The route would again be over the frozen Yalu River, in the coldest, darkest part of the year.

## SAINT ANDREW KIM

By this time the three boys who had been sent to the Paris Missions seminary in Macao should have finished their studies there. Francis-Xavier, alas, had died. The other two had fared well, and it was judged expedient to think of their return. They were to be put as interpreters on two French naval vessels that were planning to visit Korean waters, with the intention of complaining about the execution of the three French nationals in 1839. The vessels were under the command of Admiral Cécille - a name that was destined to bring more sorrow than help. Andrew Kim was to accompany two French priests, one for Manchuria and one for Korea. The plan had to be changed. Andrew and the two priests eventually went to Manchuria in a Chinese junk, arriving there at the end of October 1842. Andrew and the priest for Korea, Fr Maistre, began planning to enter Korea disguised as beggars, but the Vicar Apostolic of Manchuria quashed the plan as unworkable.

Andrew then planned to go alone. At the end of the year he got himself to a place on the road to Beijing where he was likely to meet the winter embassy as it passed through from Seoul. There were frustrating delays, but he finally succeeded and met a Christian Korean named Francis Kim, from whom he learned how the persecution had raged, and that there was now a lull. On 24 January 1843 Korean Christians in the embassy said Fr Ferréol should not attempt to cross the border. Andrew had hair-raising adventures, suffering much from cold and hunger; but he had to return to his superior. Again they waited for many months. There was some consolation when, on the last day of 1843, the Vicar Apostolic of Manchuria ordained Fr Ferréol as third Vicar Apostolic of Korea. On 17 October 1844 Andrew was ordained to the diaconate.

A fortnight later the bishop, accompanied by Andrew, reached the Korean border again. They met Francis Kim as the embassy went through. Francis was insistent that no foreign missionary should attempt the crossing, but Andrew went on alone and succeeded in crossing the frozen river. He left a vivid account in Latin of his journey, through gullies and alleys, through snow-bound mountains and over frozen streams, constantly aware that he might be discovered and questioned. If he were caught, it would be impossible to hide for long the fact that that he had illegally left and re-entered the country.

At P'yöngyang he met Charles Hyön and Thomas Yi, and his journey under their guidance to Seoul was a little easier. Andrew had brought some money with him (explaining how he came by it would have been hard if he had been arrested on the way) and he soon bought a house in Seoul. He could now move about fairly easily, and Bishop Ferréol instructed him to investigate sea routes in and out of Korea. He bought a wretched little boat and gathered an ad hoc crew of inexperienced sailors. In this craft he and Charles Hyön set sail across the Yellow Sea, intending to reach Shanghai. A tremendous storm arose. They cut their masts and entrusted their souls to God. Although many ships were lost in the Yellow Sea during that storm, this damaged craft stayed afloat long enough for them to be rescued by a Cantonese ship that took them in tow... Even so they encountered pirates. When they discharged their firearms, the pirates fled.

Eventually they were towed into the anchorage at Wusung, the port of Shanghai, which was then in the first stages of becoming an international trading centre, full of sailing vessels from European nations. The strange Korean boat and the costume of the Koreans caused a sensation. Andrew recognised a British ship. Knowing about the British from his years in Macao, Hong Kong's neighbour, he called out: 'I am a Korean. I ask your protection!' The British sailors responded, and guided him to the Chinese authorities, who suggested he return to Korea by land. Andrew was having nothing to do with that idea, which would have defeated his purpose. With the help of the British officers he made his way into Shanghai and saw the British consul, who had been forewarned by Bishop Ferréol, and found a place for him to stay with a Christian family.

A few weeks later Bishop Ferréol himself arrived in Shanghai, accompanied by Fr Antoine Daveluy, who was also destined for Korea. On 17 August 1845, the Vicar Apostolic of Jiangnan - the local bishop - ordained Andrew priest.

The bishop, Fr Daveluy and Fr Kim prepared to sail for Korea. They arrived at Kanggyöng on the west coast on 12 October. A particular joy for Andrew was being able to see his mother, Ursula, again. As we have seen, his father Ignatius had been beheaded in 1839. Soon the two bishops and Andrew were established in Seoul, where they were now fairly safe so long as they did nothing to attract attention. The bishop asked Andrew to continue working at the idea of entering and leaving Korea by sea. In the spring Andrew went to the west coast of Hwanghae province, to a group of islands which was well known as a haunt of Chinese fishermen at that season. He was apprehended there by the Korean authorities in July. They took him to their provincial capital at Haeju before they put the red cord of arrest on him and took him to Seoul.

His trial took a long time. He made a good impression on his judges, who admired his manners and his education. The records hint that they had some hope of dealing leniently with him, but Admiral Cécille now arrived off the coast, and sent peremptory messages to the Korean government about the execution of the three Frenchmen in 1839. Cécille's behaviour left no hope of pardon for Andrew, against whom the most serious charge was his treasonous contacts with Europeans. He was condemned to death. The execution place was prepared on the sands of the Han, where Bishop Imbert and his two priests had been slain seven years earlier. Here Andrew was brought on 16 September 1846, stripped and prepared for decapitation. He made a brief speech, declaring he had contacted foreigners for God's sake only, and that he was dying for God. Then he charged all those present to enter eternal life with him. When all was ready he asked the soldiers if he was correctly placed for beheading. One them adjusted the tilt of his head. The young priest did not move again. His head fell at the eighth stroke.

Fearing what might happen to the body, the authorities had it dressed in a purple coat, wrapped in reed mats and buried at once, together with the head, there on the execution ground. Christians retrieved the relics forty days later.

St Andrew is the best-loved of the Korean martyrs. Not only was he the first Korean priest, only 25 years old and not yet a year in the priesthood, he was an impressive and loveable young man. Bishop Ferréol said he loved him like a son. His judges acknowledged his fine character, and pitied him for the hard life that had been his lot. It is right that his name should stand at the head of the canonised.

## Eight friends

Three days later Charles Hyön, the catechist to whom
Bishop Imbert had committed the Church, was beheaded
with the gruesome ceremonies of military display on the
sands of the Han. His father, sister, wife and son had
already been martyred. He would have surrendered himself to martyrdom in 1838, had not the Bishop and the
two French priests dissuaded him. Since then he had led
the Church bravely. He had punctiliously collected
accounts of all the martyrs, amassing the basis of documentation that would later be used for the canonisation
process. He had been in prison since 16 July, when he
was arrested with four women who happened to be in his
house at the time of the police visit.

The four women were beheaded outside the Little
West Gate the day after Charles was executed on the
sands. Susanna U was a widow of the gentry class. She
was arrested and might have been executed in 1828, but
was released because she was then pregnant. She was
however tortured, despite the unborn child. She had a
friend with her now, Teresa Kim, a widow who worked
as a household servant in Fr Andrew's household. With
them were another widow, Agatha Yi, who had run away
from home so that she could live as a Christian, and had
been baptised by Fr Pacifico; and Catherine Chöng.
Catherine had been violently beaten by her master when
she would not take part in pagan sacrifices. She ran away

from home and joined the women in Fr Andrew's house. She still bore the marks of her beating.

Three men were killed with them. Joseph Im had been the only non-Christian in his own household, not well educated, but earning his living as a merchant. One of his sons had gone with Fr Andrew to contact the Chinese fishermen off the west coast in June. On learning that they had been apprehended, Joseph, who had joined the police in the hope of helping Christians, went to Haeju to claim his son. Unsurprisingly, he was himself arrested and taken to Seoul. He was tortured with particular cruelty, being told at one time that if he made the slightest sound it would be interpreted as apostasy. Fr Andrew's charm worked on him. He suddenly declared his faith and became the second of the martyrs to be baptised in prison. (The first was Agatha Kim in 1838.)

Peter Nam, a member of the capital garrison, was arrested in July. Although a Christian by 1839, he had escaped capture, and shortly afterwards fell into sinful ways. After a while he reformed himself and undertook severe penances, such as living in an unheated room throughout the winter. He said only martyrdom could obliterate his guilt. In prison he carefully surrendered his military tally as part of his welcome for martyrdom. He asked his pagan brothers not to visit him in prison, lest they should break his determination to die.

The last of the group was Laurence Han, member of the gentry with a rather solemn mien, but an acknowledged gift of contemplative prayer. Like many of the martyrs, he thought Christian belief involved charity of something like Franciscan prodigality. He often gave away his clothes. Bishop Imbert had appointed him catechist. Arrested at the end of August, he was tortured with particular ingenuity, having his feet cut and crushed with pottery shards. In spite of this, he refused to be taken to Seoul on a pony, even though it was impossible for him to wear shoes. As a result he walked barefoot on his wounded feet for more than 50 kilometres.

All seven were beaten to death in prison. Some of them lasted a long time under the blows. When this happened it was customary for the executioners to ease their own labours by strangling the victim. This happened to Peter Nam. It was said that a strange light appeared over his body during the night of his death. The prison guards were so moved by this that they did not throw his body out in the usual way, but gave it careful burial.

## A twenty-year lull

After autumn 1846 there was a sudden lull in the execution of Christians. This must have been because of a change of heart in the palace. The queen's family was now politically less inclined to hate Christians. Then in 1849 the king died suddenly at the age of 22, leaving no son to succeed him. The queen who had come to the fore after the Year of the White Cock was now the senior dowager. She made one of the most surprising appointments of the dynasty. She called in from the island of Kanghwa an uneducated 18-year-old farmer, an outrigger of the royal clan, whose princely ancestors had been exiled there 150 years earlier. Since he was utterly unprepared for the throne, the dowager's family again took over the reins of government. Things became easier for Christians. The new king was grandson of the princess Song who had been martyred in 1801, and may have had some latent sympathy for Christianity.

Bishop Ferréol worked secretly in Seoul for eight years. In 1853 he fell ill and died, worn out by heavy work and harsh conditions. The man appointed to succeed him was Siméon Berneux. Berneux had arrived in the Orient in 1840, when for a few weeks in Macao he was given care of the two Korean students, the future martyr Andrew Kim and Thomas Ch'oe. Still in his twenties he was sent to work in Vietnam, where he spent two years in prison for his faith. His superiors transferred him against his will to Manchuria, where he was to become bishop as Pro-Vicar-Apostolic in 1854, but hardly had he been ordained, when he was appointed to Korea. It took nearly two years for him to reach Seoul. He arrived by a junk from the Yellow Sea in January 1856.

He had his own house, but a gentleman and his family also lived in it, leaving the bishop just one room, in which he slept, ate his two daily meals and said mass. He could never go out into the courtyard during the day because women hawkers and beggars might come in at any time and his red beard would have given him away as a foreigner. He dared not open a window, even in summer, and could never raise his voice above a whisper. Twice a year he visited his flock, who were mostly very poor and had tiny houses, inside which it was impossible for him to stand upright, even for mass. He would arrive at a house before daybreak and recite the breviary while the catechist listed those coming for the sacraments. He would have breakfast, hear confessions and give instruction all day long. He lay down at night dead tired. Gentlewomen would come during the night, disguised as poor women, make their confessions, hear mass at 3 in the morning and get back home before daylight, for they had to keep their faith secret from heir husbands. Baptisms, confirmations and occasionally unction followed the mass. Then he hurried to the next congregation in another house, arriving there before dawn. This pattern was repeated daily for two months every spring and autumn.

## 1866, The Year of the Red Horse

In 1857 Fr Daveluy was ordained coadjutor bishop. The church that had begun as a group of gentry was now largely a Church of the poor, but some gentlemen and their families still belonged. One of these was John Nam, who was a tutor to the royal household. When the ploughboy king died leaving no son in 1863, the senior queen dowager of the day made another bizarre decision. She appointed as king an 11-year-old boy, whose father was still alive. There were two precedents for this, however, and the protocol was for the king's father to be known as the 'Great Prince of the Palace'. He naturally functioned as regent, a man who was famous for his beautiful ink drawings of orchids, but proved to be an unpredictable schemer.

Koreans were just becoming aware of the interest being taken in them by the western powers. European ships were appearing in Korean waters. Russia was particularly worrying. Surprisingly, there were three Christian women in the palace: the Great Prince's wife, his eldest daughter, and the boy king's nanny. These three discussed the situation with John Nam, who eventually suggested to the Great Prince that he might use Bishop Berneux as a contact with the French and British governments for an alliance against Russia. It seems that the Prince asked to meet Berneux, but there were mistakes in protocol when letters were drafted. There was a delay of ten months, perhaps partly because the missionaries were hard to contact. The Great Prince was angry and called the matter off. He also had political debts to the senior Queen Dowager's family, which was anti-Christian. He

asked to meet the two bishops. They were in Seoul by the
end of January 1866, the Year of the Red Horse; but they
already knew that the Prince's intention now was to arrest
them. Bishop Berneux was arrested on 23 February. The
gory processes that led to execution were gone through
again on the Han River sands on 6 March. The bishop
was 52. With him were executed three French priests, all
in their twenties: Juste de Bretennieres, Pierre Dorie and
Louis Beaulieu. John Nam was executed outside the
Little West Gate the same day. Three days later John
Chön, a flour merchant, and Peter Ch'oe, both of whom
had edited and published Christian books, were beheaded
in the same place.

Another two days later, two Korean laymen were martyred on the Han River sands with full military ceremonial
and display of their heads. Mark Chöng the catechist was
71. He had been converted after seeing some of the martyrs of 1839 meet their deaths. Bishop Ferréol made him
chief catechist of Seoul. Alexius U was only 21. He was
something of a prodigy, passing the national examinations
in his middle teens. He had been an ardent missionary in
Hwanghae-do, the Yellow Sea Province just north of
Seoul, and by the age of 18 had brought 100 converts to
Seoul. Arrested in 1865, he had apostatised under torture,
but had returned to the Church and was arrested in the
house of John Chön.

## 8,000 MARTYRS

Bishop Daveluy and two more French priests, Luc Huin and Pierre Aumaitre, whom he had asked to surrender in the same way that Laurent Imbert had asked Frs Maubant and Chastan, were to have been executed in the same place. The palace soothsayers objected that too much blood was being shed in Seoul and this would have a bad effect on the king's wedding, which was to happen that spring. Bishop Daveluy and the priests had been arrested with him in the district 150 miles south of Seoul where Fr Andrew Kim and so many earlier martyrs had been bred, were taken back there for execution. Decapitation with display of the heads was performed at Poryŏng on Good Friday, 30 March 1866. Thus Bishop Daveluy, who became the 5th Vicar Apostolic for Korea when Bishop Berneux died, held that office for only 22 days. With him also were martyred Luke Hwang, a catechist who had helped him with translation work, and another catechist, Joseph Chang.

Ten other names appear among the canonised for the Year of the Red Horse. Catechist Peter Yu was beaten to death in P'yŏngyang on 17 February. On the day of Bishop Daveluy's death a farmer named Thomas Son was strangled at Kongju. Seven men were beheaded in Chŏnju, the south-western provincial capital, on 13 December:

Bartholomew Chöng, of the gentry class; farmers Peter Cho and 20-year-old Peter Chöng; catechists Peter Son and 20-year-old Peter Han; and Peter Yi. Peter Cho's 18-year-old son, Joseph Cho, was beaten to death the day before. Another catechist, John Yi, was beheaded in the south-eastern city of Taegu on 21 January 1867.

These names from the 1860s are woefully unrepresentative. The choice of those canonised in 1984 depended on the collection of evidence of the standard required for the canonical process. Not only are there no women among them, though large numbers of housewives and mothers were killed, but these saints of the Year of the Red Horse form only a tiny selection from what are thought to be have been about 8,000 martyrs who died between 1866 and 1886. Few Churches can muster such a roll.

Persecution continued for several years. Families that suffered in 1801 and 1839 continued to suffer until the early 1870s. Among them were a son, grandson and two great grandsons of Peter Yi who took Chinese books to the Hermitage group in 1775 - four generations of martyrs in one family. Long after persecutions ceased, priests continued to live and work in secret. Only in 1886, when the first Franco-Korean treaty was signed, did the law relax.

## Princess Mary

When Gustave Mutel became Vicar Apostolic in 1891, the Great Prince of the Palace was still alive. It was no longer a crime to be a Christian, and the new bishop was approached by the Great Prince's wife, asking for baptism. This proved impractical because as head of the palace household she was in charge of preparing food for the ancestral sacrifices. The situation changed when in 1896 she retired from the headship because of her age (she was 78). The bishop visited her after dark on 11 October and baptised her as Mary in the house of one of her palace ladies. On 6 September 1897 he visited her again for her confession and first Holy Communion. It was also her last communion, for she died four months later on 8 January 1898. Her husband, who had started and organised the greatest of the persecutions, died on 22 February. Some time before he had sent a small gift to Bishop Mutel, together with an ambiguous message saying he regretted what he had done to the Christians and that he had been deceived.

## The martyrs' heritage

In the days of the martyrs there were no separate Korean words for 'Catholicism' and 'Christianity'. The Chinese name for Christianity, devised by the great Mateo Ricci in the 16th century, served for both. It meant, literally, 'the God Doctrine'. Belief in one almighty and loving Creator God was indeed the crucial subject on which the martyrs were most frequently questioned and for which they were derided during their trials. They died for their belief in God and salvation by the blood of Christ. The Christian virtues they most prized were humility, love, and care for the poor.

When the Churches of the Reformation began their missionary work in Korea after 1882, all of them save the Anglicans introduced a different word for God and chose to call their teaching not 'God Doctrine' but 'Jesus Doctrine'. Thus Korean Protestants came to think of the Catholic martyrs as having died for a different religion. Some wise Protestant missionaries, however, expressed great reverence for the martyrs, and today Korean Christians all increasingly see themselves as their heirs. In the 1960s the Catholic Church in Korea agreed to use the word for God preferred by Protestants.

In 1984 Pope John Paul II visited Korea to celebrate the second centenary of the baptism of Peter Yi in Beijing and the birth of the Korean Church. On 6 May at the Han River sands where St Laurent Imbert, St Andrew Kim and many others had suffered and died, he canonised 103 martyrs: 3 French bishops, 7 French priests, 46 Korean men and 47 Korean women. It was the first canonisation ever performed outside Rome.

The calendar of saints used by the Catholic Church now contains a commemoration on 20 September of 'Saint Andrew Kim Taegön, Saint Paul Chöng Hasang, and their Companions, Martyrs'. They are remembered at altars all over the world.

# FLOWERING OF THE CHURCH IN KOREA
## THE FRUIT OF THE HEROISM OF THE MARTYRS

*Pope John Paul II visited South Korea in 1984. On leaving Seoul Cathedral on Sunday morning, 6th May, the Holy Father went to Youido Square where he celebrated Mass and canonized 103 Korean Martyrs in the presence of an estimated more than half a million people.*

### Korean Martyrs inscribed in the list of Saints

"Today it is given to me, the Bishop of Rome and Successor of Saint Peter - In that Apostolic See, to participate in the jubilee of the Church on Korean soil. I have already spent several days in your midst as a pilgrim, fulfilling as Bishop and Pope my service to the sons and daughters of the beloved Korean nation. Today's Liturgy institutes the culminating point of this pastoral service.

For behold: through this liturgy of Canonization the Blessed Korean Martyrs are inscribed in the list of the Saints of the Catholic Church. These are true sons and daughters of your nation and they are joined by a number of missionaries from other lands. They are your ancestors, according to the flesh, language, and culture. At the same time they are your fathers - and mothers in the faith, a faith to which they bore witness by the shedding of their blood. From the thirteen-year-old Peter Yu to the seventy-two-year-old Mark Chong, men and women, clergy and laity, rich and poor, ordinary people and nobles, many of them descendants of earlier unsung martyrs they all gladly died for the sake of Christ.

Listen to the last words of Teresa Kwon, one of the early, martyrs: "Since the Lord of Heaven is the Father of all mankind and the Lord of all creation, how can you ask me to betray him? Even in this world anyone who betrays his own father or mother will not be forgiven. All the more may I never betray him who is the Father of us all."

A generation later, Peter Yu's father Augustine firmly declares: "Once having known God. I cannot possibly betray him." Peter Cho goes even further and says: "Even supposing that one's own father committed a crime, still one cannot disown him as no longer being one's father. How then can I say that I do not know the heavenly Lord Father who is so good?

And what did the seventeen-year-old Agatha Yi say when she and her younger brother were falsely told that their parents had betrayed the faith? Whether my parents betrayed or not is their affair. As for us, we cannot betray the Lord of heaven whom we have always served.' Hearing this, six other adult Christians freely delivered themselves to the magistrates to be martyred. Agatha, her parents and those other six are all being canonized today. In addition, there are countless other unknown. humble martyrs who no less faithfully and bravely served the Lord.

## Like unto Christ

The Korean Martyrs have borne witness to the crucified and risen Christ. Through the sacrifice of their own lives they have become like Christ in a very special way. The words of Saint Paul the Apostle could truly have been spoken by them: We are "always carrying in the body the death of Jesus so that the life of Jesus may also be manifested in our bodies. We are always being given up to death for Jesus' sake; so that the life of Jesus may be manifested in our mortal flesh." *(2 Cor 4:10-11)*.

The death of the martyrs is similar to the death of Christ on the Cross, because like his, theirs has become the beginning of new life. This new life was manifested not only in themselves - in those who underwent death for Christ- but it was also extended to others. It became the leaven of the Church as the living community of disciples and witnesses to Jesus Christ. "The blood of martyrs is the seed of Christians": this phrase from the first centuries of Christianity is confirmed before our eyes.

Today the Church on Korean soil desires in a solemn way to give thanks to the Most Holy Trinity for the gift of the Redemption. It is of this gift that Saint Peter writes: "You were ransomed... not with perishable things such as silver or gold, but with the precious blood of Christ" *(I Pt 1:18-19)*. To this lofty price, to this price of the Redemption, your Church desires, on the basis of the witness of the Korean Martyrs, to add an enduring witness of faith, hope and charity.

Through this witness may Jesus Christ be ever more widely known in your land: the crucified and risen Christ. Christ, the Way and the Truth and the Life, Christ, true God: the Son of the living God. Christ, true man: the Son of the Virgin Mary."

*(Extracts from the Homily of John Paul II at the canonization of the Korean Martyrs, 6th May 1984)*

# 103 MARTYRS OF KOREA
## CANONISED 6 MAY 1984

| No. Name (Age) | Notes (Numbers refer to list) |
|---|---|

*Decapitation with display, Han River sands, Seoul 16 September 1846*

. Kim Taegön/Andrew (25)     First Korean priest. Son of 41, nephew of 57. Gentry class.

*Beheaded outside Little West Gate, Seoul 22 September 1839*

. Chöng Hasang/ Paul (44)     Catechist. Son of 49, brother of 54. Gentry class.

*Died in the Criminal Court Prison, Seoul 25 November 1838*

. Yi Hoyöng/ Peter (35)     Catechist. Brother of 7. Gentry class.

*Beaten to death, Police Prison, Seoul 20/21 May 1839*

. Chöng Kukpo/ Protase (40)     Apostatised, then gave himself up. Gentry class.

*Beheaded outside Little West Gate, Seoul 24 May 1839*

. Kim Agi/ Agatha (52)     Widow. 'Agi' means 'daughter' and is not a name.

. Pak Agi/ Anna (56)

. Yi/ Agatha (55)     Widow. Sister of 3.

. Kim Öbi/ Magdalene(65)     Widow.

. Yi Kwanghön/ Augustine (52)Catechist. Husband of 26, father of 58, brother of 21. Gentry.

0. Han Agi/ Barbara (47)     Widow.

1. Pak Hüisun/ Lucy (38)     Virgin. Sister of 25. Palace servant.

2. Nam Myönghyök/ Damian (37)Catechist. Husband of 29.

3. Kwön Tügin/ Peter (34)     Maker of devotional articles.

*Died in the Police Prison, Seoul 26-29 May 1839.*

4. Chang Söngjip/ Joseph(53)     A herbalist.

| | | |
|---|---|---|
| **15.** | Kim/ Barbara (34) | Widow. |
| **16.** | Yi/ Barbara (14) | Granddaughter of 36, niece of 22 and 28. Gentry class. |

*Beheaded outside Little West Gate, Seoul 20 July 1839.*

| | | |
|---|---|---|
| **17.** | Kim/ Rose (55) | |
| **18.** | Kim Söngim/ Martha (49) | Gave herself up. |
| **19.** | Yi Maeim/ Theresa (51) | Sister-in law of 36, aunt of 22 and 28 Gentry class. |
| **20.** | Kim Changgüm/ Anna (50) | Widow. |
| **21.** | Yi Kwangnyöl/John (44) | Brother of 9, brother-in law of 26, uncle of 58. Gentry class. |
| **22.** | Yi Yönghüi/Magdalene (30) | Virgin. Daughter of 36, sister of 28, niece of 19, aunt of 16. |
| **23.** | Kim/ Lucy (21) | Virgin. Gave herself up. |
| **24.** | Wön Kwiim/ Maria (21) | Virgin. Seamstress. |

*Beheaded outside Little West Gate, Seoul 3 September 1839*

| | | |
|---|---|---|
| **25.** | Pak K'ünagi/ Maria (53) | Sister of 11. 'K'ünagi' ('eldest daughter') is not a name. |
| **26.** | Kwön Hüi/ Barbara(45) | Wife of 9, mother of 58, sister-in-law of 21. |
| **27.** | Pak Hujae/ John (40) | Straw shoe maker. |
| **28.** | Yi Chönghüi/ Barbara (40) | Widow. Daughter of 36, sister of 22, niece of 19, aunt of 16. |
| **29.** | Yi Yönhüi/ Maria (35) | Wife of 12. |
| **30.** | Kim Hyoju/ Agnes (23) | Virgin. Sister of 44. |

*Died in the Criminal Court Prison, Seoul 12 September 1839*

| | | |
|---|---|---|
| **31.** | Ch'oe Kyönghwan/ Francis (34) | Catechist. His son Yangöp (Thomas was 2nd Korean priest. |

*Decapitation with display, Han River sands, Seoul 21 September 1839*

| | | |
|---|---|---|
| **32.** | Laurent Imbert (43) | 2nd Vicar Apostolic (French bishop) |

| 33. | Pierre Maubant (35) | French priest. |
| 34. | Jacques Chastan (35) | French priest. |

*Beheaded outside Little West Gate, Seoul 22 September 1839*

| 35. | Yu Chin'gil/ Augustine (48) | Father of 48. Professional class. |

*Beheaded outside Little West Gate, Seoul 26 September 1839*

| 36. | Hö Kyeim/ Magdalene (66) | Mother of 22 and 28. |
| 37. | Nam Igwan/ Sebastian (59) | Catechist. Husband of 51. |
| 38. | Kim/ Julietta (55) | Virgin. Palace servant. |
| 39. | Chön Kyönghyöp/ Agatha (52) | Virgin. Palace servant. |
| 40. | Cho Sinch'öl/ Charles (46) | Husband of 70, son-in-law of 50 and 64. |
| 41. | Kim Chejun/ Ignatius (43) | Catechist. Father of 1. |
| 42. | Pak Pongson/ Magdalene (43) | Widow. |
| 43. | Hong Kümju/ Perpetua (35) | Widow. |
| 44. | Kim Hyoim/ Columba (25) | Virgin. Sister of 30. |

*Died in prison, Seoul September 1839.*

| 45. | Kim/ Lucy (70) | Nicknamed 'Hunchback'. |

*Died in prison, Seoul September-October 1839.*

| 46. | Yi/ Catherine (56) | Widow. Mother of 47. |
| 47. | Cho/ Magdalene (32) | Virgin. Daughter of 46. |

*Strangled in the Police Prison, Seoul 31 October 1839.*

| 48. | Yu Taech'öl/ Peter (12) | Son of 35. Professional class. Youngest in the canonised list. |

*Died in prison, Seoul 23 November 1839*

| 49. | Yu/ Cecilia (78) | Mother of 2 and 54. Gentry class. |

*Beheaded outside Little West Gate, Seoul 29 December 1839*

| 50. | Ch'oe Ch'anghüp/ Peter (52) | Husband of 64, father of 70, father-in-law of 40. Professional. |
| 51. | Cho Chüngi/ Barbara (57) | Wife of 37. Gentry class. |
| 52. | Han Yöngi/ Magdalene (55) | Widow. Mother of 67. |
| 53. | Hyön Kyöngnyön/ Benedicta (45) | Catechist. Sister of 72. Seamstress. Professional class. |

| 54. | Chŏng Chŏnghye/ Elisabeth (42) | Virgin. Daughter of 49, sister of 2. Gentry class. |
| 55. | Ko Suni/ Barbara (41) | Wife of 62. |
| 56. | Yi Yŏngdŏk/ Magdalene (27) | Virgin. Sister of 66. Gentry class. |

*Strangled in the Police Prison, Seoul 9 January 1840*

| 57. | Kim/ Theresa (44) | Aunt of 1. |
| 58. | Yi/ Agatha (17) | Virgin. Daughter of 9 and 26, niece of 21. |

*Strangled in the Police Prison, Seoul 30 January 1840*

| 59. | Min Kükka/ Stephen (53) | Catechist. Gentry class. |

*Strangled in the Police Prison, Seoul 23 January 1840*

| 60. | Chŏng Hwagyŏng/ Andrew (33) | Catechist. |

*Beaten to death, Seoul 31 January - 1 February 1840*

| 61. | Hŏ Im/ Paul (45) | Soldier. |

*Beheaded, Tang-kogae, Seoul 31 January 1840*

| 62. | Pak Chongwŏn/ Augustine (48) | Catechist. Husband of 55. Professional class. |
| 63. | Hong Pyŏngju/ Pete (42) | Catechist. Brother of 68. Gentry class |
| 64. | Son Sobyŏk/ Magdalene (39) | Wife of 50, mother of 70. |
| 65. | Yi Kyŏngi/ Agatha (27) | Virgin. |
| 66. | Yi Indŏk/ Maria (22) | Virgin. Sister of 56. |
| 67. | Kwŏn Chini/ Agatha (21) | Daughter of 52. Apostatised and recanted. |

*Beheaded, Tang-kogae, Seoul 1 February 1840*

| 68. | Hong Yŏngju/ Paul (39) | Catechist. Brother of 63. |
| 69. | Yi Munu/ John (31) | Catechist. Gentry class. Companion of Fr Maubant. |
| 70. | Ch'oe Yŏngi/ Barbara (22) | Daughter of 50 and 64, wife of 40. |

*Strangled in prison, Seoul 29 April 1841*

| 71. | Kim Sŏngu/ Antony (46) | Catechist. |

*Decapitation with display, Han River sands, Seoul 19 September 1846*

**72.** Hyön Söngmun/ Charles (49)    Catechist. Professional class.

*Strangled or beaten to death in the Police Prison, Seoul 20 September 1846*

**73.** Nam Kyöngmun/ Peter (50)    Soldier. Professional class.

**74.** Han Ihyöng/ Laurence (47)    Catechist. Gentry class.

**75.** U Surim/ Susanna (43)    Widow. Gentry class.

**76.** Im Ch'ibaek/ Joseph (42)    Policeman.

**77.** Kim Imi/ Theresa (35)    Virgin.

**78.** Yi Kannan/ Agatha (32)    Widow.

**79.** Chöng Ch'öryöm/ Catherine (29)

*Beaten to death, P'yöngyang 17 February 1866*

**80.** Yu Chöngnyul/ Peter (29)    Farmer.

*Decapitation with display, Han River sands, Seoul 6 March 1866*

**81.** Siméon Berneux (52)    4th Vicar Apostolic (French bishop)

**82.** Juste de Bretenières (28)    French priest.

**83.** Pierre Dorie (27)    French priest.

**84.** Louis Beaulieu (26)    French priest.

*Beheaded outside Little West Gate, Seoul 6 March 1866*

**85.** Nam Chongsam/ John (49)    Royal secretary of the 3rd grade.

*Beheaded outside Little West Gate, Seoul 9 March 1866*

**86.** Chön Changun/ John (55)    Flour merchant.
                             Published Catholic books.

**87.** Ch'oe Hyöng/ Peter (52)    Published Catholic books.

*Decapitation with display, Han River sands, Seoul 11 March 1866*

**88.** Chöng Üibae/ Mark (71)    Catechist.

**89.** U Seyöng/ Alexius (21)    Apostatised in P'yöngyang,
                             then gave himself up in Seoul.

*Decapitation with display, Kalmae-mot, Poryöng 30 March 1866*

**90.** Antoine Daveluy (49)    5th Vicar Apostolic (French bishop).

**91.** Luc Huin (30)    French priest.

**92.** Pierre Aumaitre (29)      French priest.

**93.** Chang Chugi/ Joseph (63)      Catechist.

**94.** Hwang Söktu/ Luke (53)      Catechist. Helped Bishop Daveluy in translation work.

*Strangled, Kongju 30 March 1866*

**95.** Son Chasön/ Thomas (22)      Farmer.

*Beheaded, Chönju 13 December 1866*

**96.** Chöng Munho/ Bartholomew (65) Gentry class.

**97.** Cho Hwasö/ Peter (51)      Father of 102. Farmer.

**98.** Son Sönji/ Peter (46)      Catechist.

**99.** Yi Myöngsö/ Peter (45)

**100.** Han Wönsö/ Peter (Joseph) (20) Catechist. Farmer.

**101.** Chöng Wönji/ Peter (20)      Farmer.

*Beaten to death, Chönju 12 December 1886*

**102.** Cho Yunho/ Joseph (18)      Son of 97. Farmer.

*Beheaded, Taegu 21 January 1867*

**103.** Yi Yunil/ John (43)      Catechist.

The first Korean item presented to the British Museum Library i Additional Manuscript 14054. It is a copy of the Chinese Lord's Praye transcribed in Korean script by Paul Yun who was martyred in 1795 His cause for canonisation is being promoted by the diocese of Suwön.